NORTHERN
HIDEAWAYS

Introduction by Julia Jamrozik

NORTHERN
HIDEAWAYS
Canadian Cottages and Cabins

images
Publishing

CONTENTS

Introduction Julia Jamrozik

Few experiences are more quintessential for many Canadians than spending time at a cottage: a home away from home surrounded by nature. The retreat, be it a ski chalet, a boathouse, or a cabin in the woods, takes on an almost mythical significance and provides a cherished escape to be shared with family and friends.

Beyond their role as refuge, the hideaways presented in this book from Canada's east coast to the west share a simple contemporary architectural aesthetic, clean lines, and a pared down palette of natural materials. They provide warmth, comfort, and luxury, from which to experience slivers of the vast Canadian landscape in all seasons. Amplifying relationships to the outdoors, by careful orientation, crafting fluid boundaries between inside and outside, and framing views, these holiday homes curate the experience of nature for their inhabitants.

Through moments of play and moments of repose, spaces for gathering and spaces for intimacy, the hideaways are designed for experience. Here is a warm minimalism that is not afraid to borrow from the vernacular, one that does not pretend to be seamless with its surroundings but that also doesn't proclaim a bold formal independence. These are buildings that speak to and learn from their context, relying on the setting as counterpoint and counterpart.

For those with the means to do so, the precious moments of retreat to commune with nature outside the city are all the more poignant in our time of climate crisis. Many of the projects presented work with passive and active systems to minimize environmental impact, yet their very existence in the landscape also prompts questions of the use of the land and who gets to settle and occupy it and for what purpose. The proximity and attention to the cycles of the seasons, the flora and fauna, the specificity of topography, and the expansive views, bring an embodied consciousness of the richness and the robustness but also of the fragility of the natural environment. The hope is that the cottage experience will lead to moments of pleasure but also to heightened awareness and ecological stewardship for generations to come.

Julia Jamrozik is a Canadian designer, artist and educator. Working in collaboration with Coryn Kempster, their multi-disciplinary practice operates at a variety of scales, from temporary installations to permanent public artworks and architectural projects. Their academic research focuses on the role of play in the built environment and alternative methods of documentation as a form of historic preservation. They are the authors of *Growing up Modern: Childhoods in Iconic Homes* (Birkhäuser, 2021). In 2018 the Architectural League of New York honored their work with the Architectural League Prize for Young Architects and Designers.

FBM

Indian Point, Nova Scotia

MAY HOUSE

May House is located east of Mahone Bay on Nova Scotia's South Shore. The place has always been shaped by the ocean. Its sheltered waters were once an important summertime Mi'kmaq settlement. Later, the settler fishing industry created a seascape of wharfs, boatsheds, and fishing vessels. Now the context includes an eclectic mix of holiday homes as people enjoy living, rather than working, by the sea.

It was the ocean that first attracted the owners to Nova Scotia from Frankfurt, Germany. Incrementally they have made the community their summer home as a counterpoint to their busy lives working between Germany and New York. The design quietly celebrates the simple pleasures of sunlight, fresh air, and nature. Designed to be both in and of the landscape, the house choreographs the site, negotiating the gentle grade between land and sea.

May House creates a sense of prospect and refuge within its modest program. A triple-glazed curtainwall and large south-facing overhangs support a passive solar strategy. Untreated torrefied wood boards and stone cladding ensure the long-term durability of the home. These materials also reflect the passage of time as they gently gray in the salt air.

The floor plan is divided into dwelling and utility areas. The interior features a thick band of storage along the entry side of the home. The stone hearth and terrace extend from inside to outside to connect with the site and expand the home's livable areas while the large overhangs protect the home from the weather. Inside or out, owners and guests can enjoy the beauty of the Nova Scotian landscape.

This home was designed through extensive ongoing consultation with, and participation among, the owners, builder, engineers, and architect. The design draws inspiration from the landscape and local building materials. It comfortably responds to both client-driven desires, builder input, and a thoughtful relationship to nature.

The design quietly celebrates the simple pleasures of sunlight, fresh air, and nature.

SMITH HOUSE

MacKay-Lyons Sweetapple Architects
Upper Kingsburg, Nova Scotia

Smith House is a vacation home located on the Atlantic coast of Nova Scotia, adjacent to the architect's farm (Shobac). The home consists of three pavilions on a two-acre site spanning from a salt pond on the east to bold oceanfront on the west. The Smiths' initial request was for a house design that referred to a 400-year-old granite ruin, adjacent to the new structure.

The house is perched on a stone acropolis, like a ruin, protected by Corten steel plate roofs. The stone plinth is constructed of local granite, brought to the place by retreating glaciers during the last ice age, over 15,000 years ago.

The day pavilion contains the social gathering functions of the dwelling—kitchen, dining, and living—and is almost completely glazed, emphasizing the ocean horizon, and views to the surrounding hills, cliffs, and buildings. The polished concrete floor is contrasted by the white ash plywood ceiling. Two totemic elements punctuate the day pavilion: a long, free-standing kitchen core and island, clad in white ash boards; and a large granite fireplace, with a mantle stone that still carries the marks of its making. Tables are custom designed for the house. A granite wine cellar is hidden beneath the kitchen, accessed by a secret white ash trap door and staircase. Access to the night pavilion is via a granite plinth. The bedroom is a minimalist white wooden volume, with a sunken, white ash 'vessel' below.

Perfect for a relaxing holiday, the owners partake of stunning ocean panoramas, while unwinding in the stylish interior, basking in the warmth of a fire in the imposing fireplace.

The Smiths' initial request was for a house design that referred to a 400-year-old granite ruin, adjacent to the new structure.

CAP ST-MARTIN
RÉSIDENCE

Bourgeois / Lechasseur architects
Potton, Quebec

Located at the end of a long and winding road, this beautiful second home makes the most of its lakeside location, with views over the still waters and stretching across to the wooded hills beyond.

The form of the house was a request by the clients, who desired a 'barnhouse' style, an architectural influence that pays homage to the region's long farm buildings. The brief was for a warm second home designed to be a gathering place that offers a great view of the natural surroundings. The design moves toward a simple and elongated shape, characterized by a contemporary reinterpretation of the archetypal barn form.

The main heart of the residence was inspired by a wish for a spacious, bright and lake-oriented 'great room' in which to gather. This central room that hosts the living spaces is quite surprising. Its two long glass façades offer a contrast between the view of the forest and the view of the lake. The room provides plenty of natural light all day long, so you literally feel like you're outside. The cathedral ceiling, covered with wood, gives the place a softer feel.

The pure lines and refined treatment of the façades promote integration into the region's natural and built landscape. Upstairs, the master bedroom with its own patio offers a breathtaking view across the water.

The design brief for a warm holiday home that offers great views of the surrounding natural landscape has been successfully achieved.

Its two long glass façades offer a contrast between the view of the forest and the view of the lake.

COTTAGE ON THE POINT

Paul Bernier Architecte
Lanaudière, Quebec

When asked to completely renovate a holiday cottage that had been in the family for forty years, Paul Bernier Architecte designed a renovation that would expand the log cabin, making it an open, fluid, and bright space that took advantage of the beautiful views overlooking the lake.

The designers were mindful to be respectful of the original structure, electing to add an extension on the top, allowing the original log cabin to remain clearly visible while the new addition is contemporary in style.

The original cabin, on its stone foundation, is rustic, made of stone and logs with its sloping roof with wide overhangs. This stone base, anchored on the rock cap from which the site is made, helps to integrate the cabin into its natural environment. The addition is a clean and monolithic volume but whose material (wood) and color echo those of the original cottage.

The beautiful old massive stone fireplace has been restored and is now visible on all sides, right in the center of the space. The new staircase is light and minimalistic. It was also important to preserve the cathedral ceiling of the old cottage, even if a floor was to be added above. To do this, the old roof, which was frail, was completely removed and replaced by a Douglas fir structure replicating the slope and supporting the new floor. Outside, the old roof profile of the original cabin is still visible.

Adding a new story opened up a new and exceptional view of the lake and an opening to the sky that did not exist on the ground floor. This observation post has been given to the master bedroom. From their bed, the owners have a breathtaking view of the point with its beautiful tall pines, as well as the lake and the starry night sky. The addition on the roof also serves to illuminate the ground floor through a large vertical opening on the east side. Thus, the heart of the cottage on the ground floor, which would normally be darker, is illuminated with natural light.

The new screened porch installed on the south side, and fitted with two skylights discreetly inserted into the structure, offers another place to enjoy the outdoors in a space bathed in the natural light that reflects on the water.

From their bed, the owners have a breathtaking view of the point with these beautiful tall pines, as well as the lake and the starry night sky.

GRAND-PIC
CHALET

APPAREIL architecture
Austin, Quebec

Inspired by traditional shapes and the surrounding nature, this chalet design is a unique structure tailor-made for its residents. The owners wanted a warm space, fit to host family and friends, in harmony with the environment, a space that breathes fresh air and replenishment. Grand-Pic Chalet offers, through simplicity and sober physicality, a unique experience of symbiosis between nature and architecture.

The design of the cottage results from a sensitive reading of the magnificent woods in which it is located. Before even starting to imagine the project, the objective was to be guided and inspired by the terrain's characteristics. Each move was influenced by a desire to optimize the space's intrinsic qualities.

The interior plane is organized around a central technical core. On the ground floor, the partitions were rendered minimally, freeing the living spaces. The kitchen, partially integrated with the core, benefits from a large storage space. On the second floor, the central core prolongs itself, this time into a dormitory zone for guests. Interior openings, overlooking the ground-floor spaces, accentuate the influx of light and create a link between the two levels.

In contrast to the black monochrome exterior, the interior overflows with light through its openings, and through the brightness of its materials. The omnipresence of light wood tinges the interior light, giving it similar characteristics to the light under the nearby vegetal cover. The wood's texture on all walls and ceilings of the interior envelope allows the shape of the vernacular-inspired main interior volume to be accentuated.

The objective of creating a sober and warm space for the owners was made possible through an architecture steeped in simplicity. As much through its volume and its design as through its exterior and interior coverings, Grand-Pic Chalet offers a timeless construction inspired by Nordic traditions.

Grand-Pic Chalet offers a timeless construction inspired by Nordic traditions.

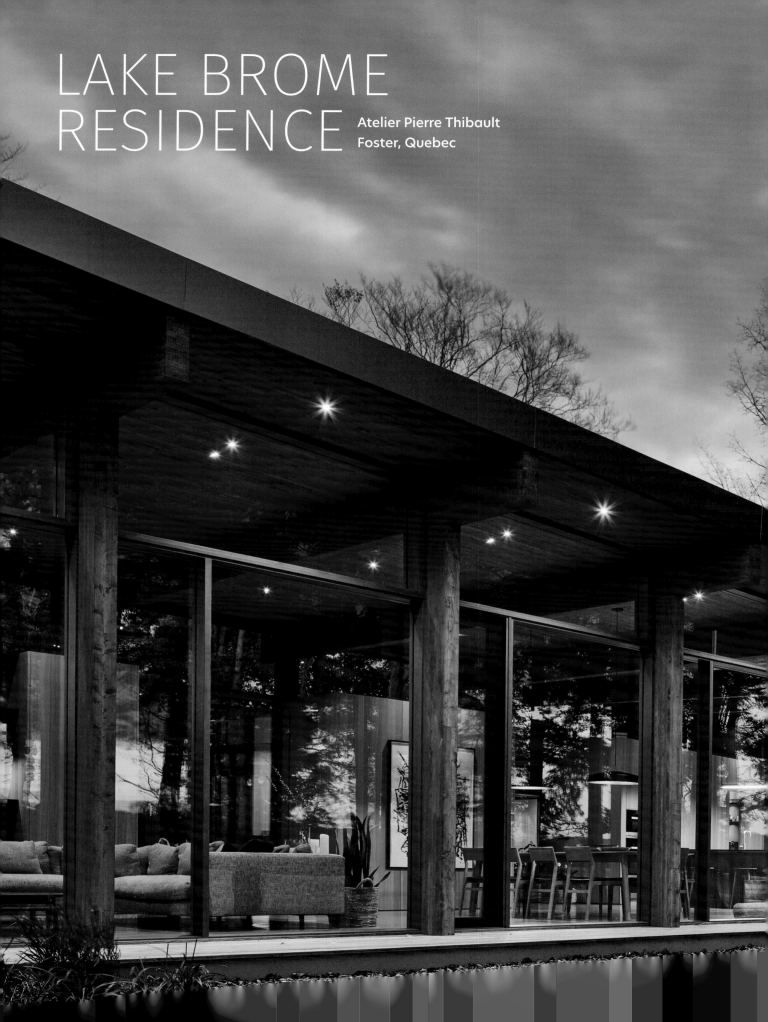

LAKE BROME RESIDENCE

Atelier Pierre Thibault
Foster, Quebec

Situated on the majestic titular lake in the Southern Eastern Townships, Lake Brome Residence was first inspired by a large, outdoor, covered terrace where the family could live immersed in nature. The single-level dwelling, designed with floor-to-ceiling windows, takes full advantage of the sweeping lakeside views and surrounding mountainous landscape.

The challenge for the designers was to orient the house on its relatively small lot toward the sublime panorama of the lake without compromising the privacy of the occupants. The chosen strategy was to create a single-story project unfolding into two wings linked by a glass connection.

Composed of wood and stone walls, Lake Brome Residence relies on the durability and nobility of natural materials in order to integrate in a refined, elegant and yet modest way into its environment. At key moments, dazzling visual openings cross the house to project the gaze toward the lake.

The design was a joint collaboration with Atelier Pierre Thibault and Montreal-based manufacturer of premium hardwood furniture, Kastella, who also designed a custom-length bench and outdoor table that take pride of place in the covered outdoor eating area.

The design-savvy clients selected walnut with a water-based finish as the primary, interior material. The warm, caramel tones of the paneled walls and integrated case goods add depth and character to the new construction.

The highly functional kitchen includes two strategically placed 10-foot islands that maximize the lakeside views while maintaining the welcoming nature of the home. This elegant residence shines with its refinement, which is gradually revealed. The color chosen for the wood interior coating is rich, achieving a harmonious balance in the perceived amplitude of the space: this dark color on the ceiling and the wooden window frames give a cozy atmosphere to the interior rooms while interacting with the color of the tree trunks surrounding the house.

At key moments, dazzling visual openings cross the house to project the gaze toward the lake.

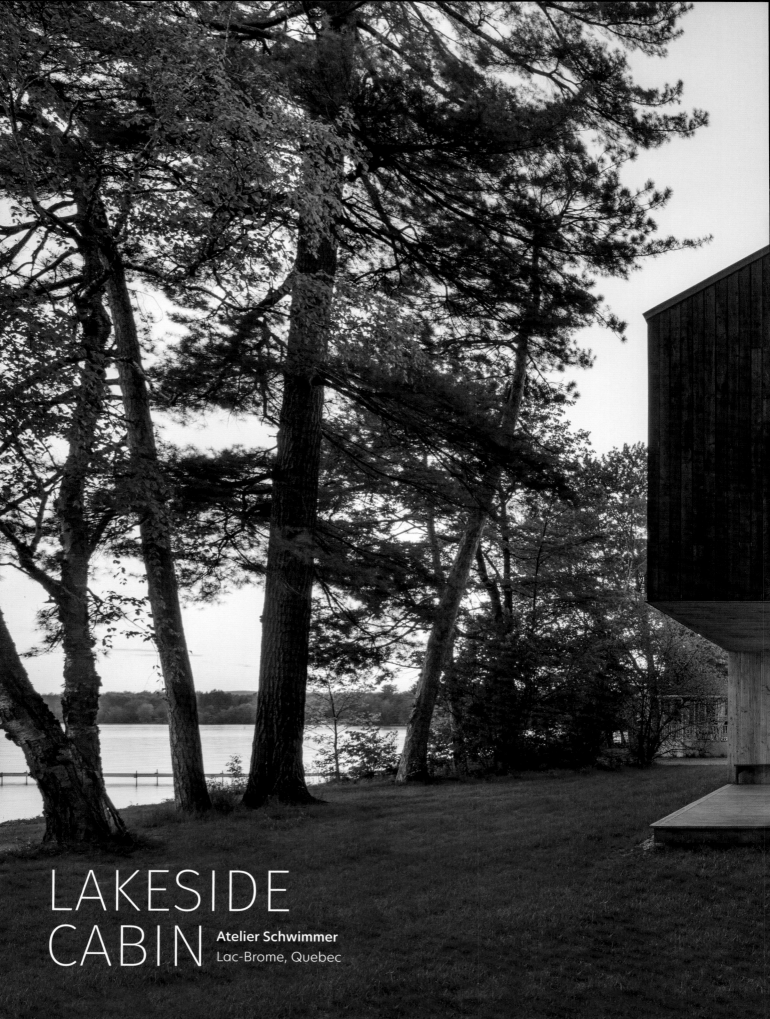

LAKESIDE CABIN

Atelier Schwimmer
Lac-Brome, Quebec

Two brothers approached architect Alex Schwimmer to request a new vacation home to be built on the shores of Lac-Brome, near a small town in the Eastern Townships. The new structure is set among classical nineteenth-century houses and more recently built modest holiday cottages. Lakeside Cabin becomes a place to share time with friends and embrace outdoor activities away from the fast-paced life in the city.

Bisected by a vertical atrium that opens out to the lake, the essence of the design is a concrete floor with a fireplace at its center that creates a place to mingle, and a place to relish the possibilities and pleasures of holidays, whether it be skiing, snowshoeing, fishing, eating together, playing board games, or watching movies. Participants (the more, the merrier) share the space and enjoy the views.

Conceived as an archetypal house, the building has three entrances, forming a loggia at the entrance and at the back, and a covered terrace on the side. The cabin's central focus is an atrium that opens to the outdoors. The design was developed around a fireplace set beside a triple-height area that makes it visible from everywhere within the cabin thus generating a canyon of hospitality. Located in the center of a concrete slab floor on the ground floor, the fireplace divides the open space into areas of various spatial qualities. On both sides of the canyon, glazed walls offer views on the outdoors. Traversing the canyon on the second floor is a bridge that creates more common space. Four bedrooms open onto the bridge.

The tension rooted in the site stems from urban-size width that squeezes the cabin between a number of others houses on its sides and its infinite view over the lakefront sheltered by a natural wall created by the tree-filled hill at the back. The exterior cladding is made of larch treated with two methods. Charred planks directly face the elements and natural oil protects the recessed, less exposed planks. This play of dark and light increases the singular aspect of the house.

Lakeside Cabin becomes a place to share
time with friends and embrace outdoor
activities away from the fast-paced
life in the city.

LAURENTIAN
SKI CHALET

RobitailleCurtis
Saint-Donat, Quebec

This modern ski chalet forms the weekend retreat for an active family. Sitting on a steep slope of a former ski hill, from this elevation, surrounded by a dense forest of spruce, maple, beech, and birch trees, the chalet commands panoramic views over beautiful Lac Archambault.

To maintain the natural topography of the steep mountainside and to minimize the footprint of construction, the house was built on a series of western red cedar pilotis. Elevating the house allows snow and spring run-off to flow freely beneath the structure.

The home is accessed via an entry bridge. The main floor has an open plan connecting the kitchen, dining area, and living room. Spanning the length of the kitchen and dining areas is a generous bay window and window seat, which contains concealed storage. A dramatic panoramic window wall runs the full width of the bay and focuses views on the remarkable landscape beyond. High on the opposite side of the chalet, a continuous clerestory window runs the full length of the house bringing in morning light and views of the mountain above.

The kitchen features a large central island that contains a gas cooktop and a prep sink so that the host does not turn their back to the views or the family and friends they are entertaining. The kitchen's adjacency to the long window seat creates a generous and comfortable place for the family and guests to gather after a day of skiing.

The east sides of the kitchen and dining room are built into a shallow bay that articulates itself on the entry façade. The living room occupies the southern end of the home where daylight streams in from windows on three sides. A fireplace anchors the living room, while a smaller, cozy window seat with mountain views provides additional seating.

The exterior of the house is uniformly clad in dark stained white cedar siding. The chalet's thermal envelope is highly insulated and carefully detailed to minimize thermal bridging and energy consumption.

The chalet commands panoramic views over beautiful Lac Archambault.

MAISON PERCHÉE

Natalie Dionne Architecture
East Bolton, Quebec

Perched on the edge of an escarpment, this modest retreat is set on a small plateau of limited dimensions. Almost straddling the void, it runs along the top of the cliff providing a bird's-eye view of the Long Lake with the Appalachian mountains as a backdrop. Set in a rolling landscape in the Eastern Townships, Maison Perchée was conceived as a dialogue with the landscape.

This vista is apparent from the entrance porch, through a generously glazed passageway that runs right through the building. This large transparent corridor in the center of the chalet allows the inhabitants to take advantage of the surrounding nature and functions as a buffer to privatize the master suite.

The inclination of the roof provides generous height under the ceiling, allowing for the integration of large picture windows and to arrange a mezzanine dedicated to a bunkroom suite accommodating guests.

Simplicity and a limited materials pallete help to emphasize the views. Large openings frame a variety of landscapes including distant mountains with changing colors, mature hemlocks, and the small forest vegetation surrounding the chalet and the grassy plain out front. Integrated terraces amalgamate interior and exterior. The largest one, overhanging the precipice, looks toward the lake and Mont-Orford. Another, anchored to the rocky ground and nestled in a coniferous forest, provides intimate shelter as it is covered with a balcony where guests are invited to bask in the treetops. The front porch, open to the plateau and the rocky forest beyond, welcomes visitors and residents, revealing architecture through transparency.

With its oblique silhouette, its simple shape, and its refined materiality, this holiday home is ideally suited for family and friends to gather and contemplate the magnificent natural environment in which they find themselves immersed.

Set in a rolling landscape, Maison Perchée was conceived as a dialogue with the landscape.

PREFABRICATED COUNTRY HOME

Figurr Architects Collective
Ivry-sur-le-Lac, Quebec

Following the purchase of a humble country house many years ago, the owners wanted to treat themselves to a new holiday home where the space would comfortably accommodate all the new members of their family. Overlooking Lake Manitou in Ivry-sur-le-Lac, Quebec, the home is composed of five prefabricated custom modules, each approximately 50 feet (15 meters) long, that were constructed before being shipped to their final destination. The concept allowed for indoor construction under optimal working conditions.

The modular design is unique, created according to precise plans by the architect, who also happens to be one of the owners. The insulation, windows, and flooring were all assembled before shipping. Transporting the giant modules proved to be quite a challenge. The process included preparation, coordination, and navigating through country roads with ninety-degree turns in inclement weather.

Conceptualized with the vision of creating an extremely low environmental footprint, the house was built using sustainable and local materials, and the architect-owner is in the process of applying for a LEED Gold certification. The large windows capture the beauty of nature in all its glory and flood the inside with light. The direct sunshine helps in reducing both heating and lighting costs.

The natural-colored outdoor façade blends easily into the woodland décor and the opaque black accents add an artistic flair. The wood used indoors is warm and welcoming.

The house interior was designed so that each member of the family has their own personal space. The ground floor's open concept has a large kitchen and dining area where everyone enjoys cooking and eating delicious meals together, a beautiful, cozy living room space, and a three-season screened-in porch surrounded by lake and woods. The ground floor also has an atelier for painting and carpentry. The lowered lakeside deck was designed to not disturb the view of the magnificent scenery.

The house interior was designed so that each member of the family has their own personal space.

Nathalie Thibodeau architecte
Saint-Ignace-de-Loyola, Quebec

RÉSIDENCE
ST-IGNACE

Offering a place of respite, Résidence St-Ignace creates distinct experiences with its unique surroundings, allowing the resident to contemplate nature while inhabiting it. The home's openings create visual breakthroughs that magnify the environment and place architecture at the service of the landscape.

The site is naturally separated from the road by a series of mature trees, and its access is positioned to maintain this natural screen. At the heart of the project, a terrace provides access to the house and acts as a union between the two built volumes. The dark-stained grooved cedar siding marks the entrance to the residence. A long alley naturally invites visitors to the living room, where a narrow view is unveiled, revealing the river in the background. This is how the house gently reveals the landscape that surrounds it, drawing attention, and unconsciously preparing the visitor for the show to come.

Entering the open area within the home, it is finally possible to appreciate the river in all its magnitude. The generous bay windows do more than frame the landscape, they let it spill into the house allowing the viewer to appreciate its immensity. The clear ceilings and the absence of partitions amplify this feeling of space and magnitude. In dialogue with the clearing on the river, the bay window of the living room allows the resident to appreciate a landscape on a different scale, focused on the proximity and the unique characteristics of the vegetation. The two openings on the outside, placed on either side of the space, enable a sense of communion with the natural surrounds. The outdoor terraces provide the perfect perch to sit and enjoy the surrounding landscapes.

The home's openings create visual
breakthroughs that magnify the
environment and place architecture
at the service of the landscape.

THE SLENDER
HOUSE
MU Architecture
Lake Memphremagog, Quebec

Located in the beautiful region of the Eastern Townships near the United States border in Quebec, The Slender House residence unfolds in a long linear volume. Nestled on the steep shores of Lake Memphremagog, the home opens up onto a peaceful secluded bay.

The Slender House is a contemporary reinterpretation of the bungalow of the 1960s, combining tradition with elegance. This 4,500-square-foot (418-square-meter) structure is solidly anchored in the rock thanks to its numerous stone retaining walls and paved terraces. Massive dry-stacked, locally supplied granite volumes serve as bases on which rests an impressive long roof with bladelike sharp edges.

On the approach to the house, a huge glass bay window marks the entrance from which a view of the lake is immediately revealed. The austere and rough appearance of the exterior stands in contrast with the very large, bright and airy interiors of the house. Large bay windows, skylights, and immaculate white walls literally flood the space with light and offer breathtaking views of the lake. At times reaching 25 feet (7 meters) high, ceilings stretch to augment the amplitude of these living spaces. All the rooms of The Slender House are positioned to form one single linear row.

The kitchen and the built-in furniture of the fireplace that conceals the television were designed down to the smallest detail to mask all the technical aspects. The whiteness of the kitchen is revealed as an extension of the walls and ceilings while the island is born from the extension of the floors that are covered in large panels of white oak.

Setting the residence on such a steep ground necessitated the construction of numerous retaining walls offering a great opportunity to develop hanging gardens. Illuminated in the evening, this cascade of vegetation is fully appreciated from the inside and provides additional enchantment.

*The Slender House is a contemporary
reinterpretation of the bungalow of
the 1960s, combining tradition
with elegance.*

ELL HOUSE

Ravi Handa Architect + AAmp Studio
Wellington, Ontario

Ell House is designed to be a vacation home that connects the visitor to the vast surrounding landscape. Its simple lines are inspired by Prince Edward County's rural vernacular. While the gable roof is reminiscent of the region's barns, the L shape references the extensions built on farmhouses over generations.

The client's objective was to separate the private areas from the communal spaces. Therefore, each of the two wings has its own purpose—the sleeping area with its four bedrooms and two baths, and the common area where the kitchen, dining room, and living room flow seamlessly into one another. The building's form is also a technical response to the area's prevailing southwesterly winds. One wing shields the other, providing a peaceful indoor and outdoor living area. The spacious glass vestibule that connects the two structures is the first point of contact when visiting the house. You can set your luggage down in the vestibule, take in the waterfront, and enjoy a moment of relaxation and sense of arrival.

Special attention was given to the location of each opening to showcase the natural surroundings. In the common area, large sliding doors frame the courtyard and water beyond. The vast lake and rural landscape can be admired from the master bedroom or the dining room table.

In both wings, a palette of natural materials and understated colors creates an interior that's minimalistic yet inviting. To add to the common area's warmth, the kitchen, dining room, and living room share the same bright, airy space where the cathedral ceiling accentuates the openness and serves as a reminder of the house's form. The exterior's monochrome aesthetic, emphasized by its charred cedar cladding, reflects the contrasts at play with the outside world.

By virtue of its simple lines, Ell House magnifies the stark contrast of its natural setting while providing a peaceful living space that embodies the notion of shelter and encouraging its guests to connect directly with nature.

Ell House is designed to be a vacation home that connects the visitor to the vast surrounding landscape.

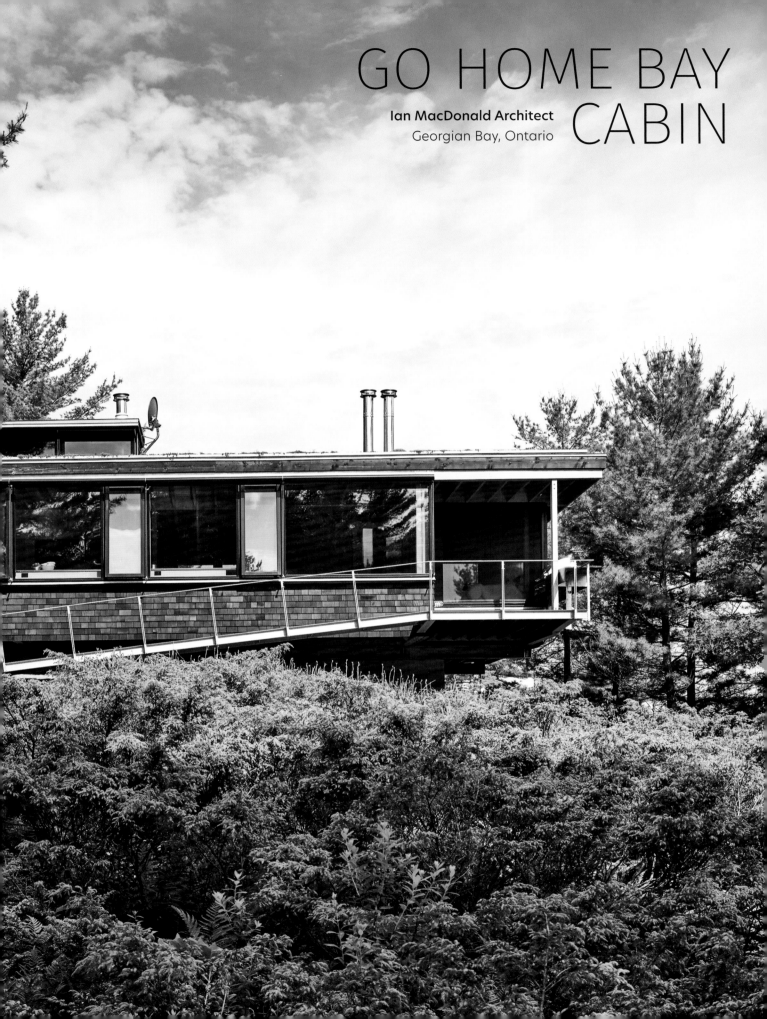

GO HOME BAY CABIN

Ian MacDonald Architect
Georgian Bay, Ontario

This modest family cabin on the Georgian Bay archipelago is a serene, sustainable place of escape. Its design responds to the cultural heritage and natural beauty of Go Home Bay, a landscape immortalized by the Group of Seven artists. Perched upon a rocky outcrop, the cabin is nearly invisible from the water—a counterpoint to the over-scaled houses increasingly common in cottage country.

The cabin stands in stark contrast to the many large object buildings that dot and dominate the landscape of the Georgian Bay archipelago. It hides itself in the landscape through thoughtful consideration of views from the water and a technical resolution of how to 'touch' the landscape lightly. While the design language is contemporary, it embodies the region's vernacular characteristics of building construction and simplicity. It is this simplicity that belies a profound connection to the surroundings that is at once stirring and peaceful.

The cabin's relationship to the landscape is about framing experience and views, and response to prevailing weather and climatic conditions. A rough-hewn fir roof spans the entire volume, with more intimate areas defined by a solid concrete thermal mass structure that provides lateral resistance and stores heat produced by the two embedded wood-burning stoves. A green roof irrigated with lake water provides evaporative cooling, which combines with ventilation through a long clerestory lantern to provide sustainable climate control. The summer heat is further tempered by sunshades integrated into the kitchen elevation, which reduce heat gain in the morning, and a long west wall of screened openings that ventilate the living and dining area, further protected by a long overhang above the adjacent deck.

The design embraces sustainable technologies to ensure that a comfortable accommodation can be achieved on this hot, backwater site without an undue expenditure of energy. Exterior shades and an irrigated green roof provide passive cooling, while large sliding glass doors and clerestory allow ample cross ventilation.

The cabin's relationship to the landscape is about framing experience and views, and response to prevailing weather and climatic conditions.

KAWAGAMA LAKE BOATHOUSE

Building Arts Architects
Dorset, Ontario

Blessed with many large lakes, it is no wonder that Canadians enjoy water activities. And many a holiday home doubles up as a boathouse. This boathouse on Kawagama Lake, built to replace an older existing structure, is tucked into a heavily forested corner of the site at the water's edge. It was designed with a particular focus: not only to provide boat storage, but a small dwelling to maximize the lake experience.

The boathouse includes a dry slip boat storage via marine railway, but also a small cabin accessed by a small bridge structure, which spans the native topography. The cabin facilities are very basic and the intent was to create a space that heightens the experience of living on the water through siting, view, sound, and smell. An outdoor fireplace sets the stage for lakeside star gazing with a large wood deck structure. The site topography and the adjacent forest were protected and strongly influenced how this building engages the site.

The site is accessible only by water and therefore the design was highly influenced by the practicality of the construction process. All systems, including the structure, were designed to be transported by small watercraft, moved, and erected by hand using only a small crew.

Materials were primarily selected for both their aesthetics and their durability and performance in freeze/thaw conditions. The architects reused as much of the lumber from the existing structure as possible, due to the challenges of bringing and removing materials to/from the site. The lower level of the boathouse was clad with wood siding salvaged from the existing structure. Douglas fir was selected for its warmth and also its ubiquitous heritage in Ontario cottage country.

The boathouse provides both seasonal storage of watercraft and waterside living. It sits gently on the site with small-diameter pier foundations and the materials used allow the building to quietly fade into the surrounding forest. On most days from almost all vantage points, the boathouse reflects the forest or lake and is challenging to identify until you are immediately in front of it. This was a fundamental requirement for the client and a defining principal of the design.

The boathouse reflects the forest or lake and is challenging to identify until you are immediately in front of it.

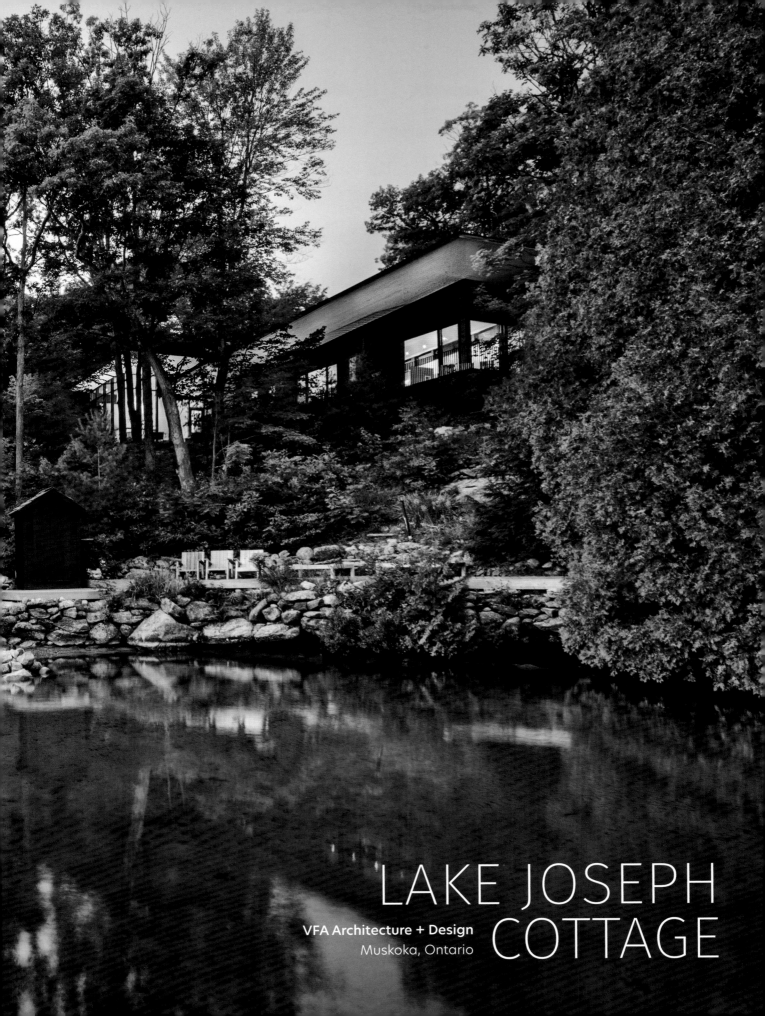

LAKE JOSEPH COTTAGE

VFA Architecture + Design
Muskoka, Ontario

Lake Joseph Cottage is located in Ontario's Muskoka region—an area long known to city-dwellers as a summer getaway and, more recently, for its rapidly developing recreation economy. Once scattered with compact summer homes tucked into the shores of its 1,600 lakes, the region now sees an influx of progressively larger and more obtrusive structures.

Lake Joseph Cottage disrupts this narrative by skillfully inserting a contemporary, year-round living space into a natural landscape. A holistic understanding of site conditions, climate, and views guided the siting of the project's three low-slung volumes, unified by a series of formally expressive overlapping hip roofs that also function as a sunshade.

A breezeway uncouples the main living space from the screened-in porch, framing a view of the lake on arrival while permitting efficient passive ventilation of the entire cottage. A naturally preserved wood façade requires little maintenance, with charred shou sugi ban framing the home in its surroundings.

The architect's interpretation of the archetypal cottage experience expresses harmony with its environment; where architecture becomes part of the landscape and respects the time-honored tradition of cottage retreating as well as the surrounding wilderness.

Lake Joseph Cottage respects the time-honored tradition of cottage retreating as well as the surrounding wilderness.

LAKE MANITOUWABING

MJMA Architecture & Design
McKellar, Ontario

RESIDENCE

The family wanted a new all-season holiday home with the goal of maximizing outdoor living and entertaining space, and the requirement of being comfortable all year round. The result is this modern structure, set back from the water's edge, that cascades over the landscape, creating a quiet presence and blending in with its surroundings.

The design needed to address the different needs of the resident in a Canadian climate. A large screened porch with retractable insect screen allows for extended outdoor enjoyment during the summer months. The site's orientation is south and west, collecting warmth, light, and views throughout the day. Deep overhangs and large glazed areas on the south and west were modeled to protect from solar buildup in summer and allow for heating gains in winter while the north and east façades are heavily opaque and highly insulated to protect from wind, and heat loss. Concrete radiant floor heating contributes to energy conservation, creating heat sinks through the day and night. A slate-gray wood fireplace provides a focal point of the sunken living room.

The client posed a unique question: "Can you design a Canadian cottage where Frank Sinatra might like to hang out?" The design pays homage to the flat roofs so typical of warmer latitude midcentury precedents, such as Palm Springs, while the interior is sleek and rich in stylish retro chic.

This is a home that will keep you stylish and snug throughout the year, even if the weather outside is frightful. One may well end up singing along with Frank: "Let it snow, let it snow."

The design needed to address the different needs of the resident in a Canadian climate.

LAKE MISSISSAUGA
COTTAGE

architects Tillmann Ruth Robinson
Kawartha Highlands, Ontario

A four-season escape for a busy young family, this Kawarthas-region cottage explores the duality of being both intimate and expansive. Located on the edge of a quiet bay at the end of a rustic gravel road, the heavily treed site is secluded upon approach, yet opens up to a dramatic Lake Mississauga vista.

Inside, the L-shaped building strikes a similar balance between privacy and openness, with grand social spaces designed to accommodate large gatherings of extended family and friends, and other, more tucked away areas introducing intimate spots to relax and recharge.

To control scale and impact on the site, the cottage is divided into two forms based on private and semiprivate functions. A horizontal wing built parallel to the shoreline skews communal and open-concept, joining a large great room with a spacious kitchen. A second, vertical volume intersects this form at a ninety-degree angle to introduce two floors of sleeping quarters. Flanking the edge of this taller volume, a glazed hallway creates a sunlit link between the cottage's two main zones, building a sense of anticipation as it approaches the sprawling great room's sublime lake view and central stone hearth.

As key elements of the project, stone and wood serve to emphasize the dialogue between architecture and nature by reflecting the building's surroundings. Along with the cottage's massing, this materiality also softens the scale of the project to create the impression of a more modest intervention. The end result is a place that feels warm, welcoming, and completely at home in its wilderness setting.

The end result is a place that feels warm, welcoming, and completely at home in its wilderness setting.

SKY HOUSE

Julia Jamrozik and Coryn Kempster
Stoney Lake, Ontario

Negotiating the steep topography of a lakeside site in the Kawartha region east of Toronto, this holiday house consists of two volumes stacked on one another. The upper volume, with a sense of openness enhanced by tall ceilings, contains living spaces and opens up toward the lake while the lower volume is more enclosed, offering warmth and coziness, and houses the sleeping quarters.

Responding to the need for accessibility for guests with disabilities, as well as thinking of the clients' ability to use the building far into the future, a study/bedroom and accessible bathroom are provided on the main level. In the main space a glazed-brick fireplace socle provides a special warm nook for the clients' daughter to snuggle with her dog.

A strong desire to minimize the ecological footprint resulted in strategic siting, minimizing impact and demand through passive strategies and generating energy through active ones. The building was sited so no old-growth trees were cut down for construction.

In addition, numerous elements were added to create a sustainable and energy-efficient home. The factory-inspired skylights of the upper volume are rotated to admit north light without heat gain while orienting the solar panels due south. The combination of vertical skylights and a fully glazed south-facing façade result in a generously daylit interior. A covered walkway shades the main wall of glass from summer sun while admitting lower winter sun to passively heat the dark-dyed concrete floor. All active systems are electric so that they can be operated by the energy generated on-site, resulting in a net-zero home.

Simple, low-maintenance, long-life materials are used on the façade, while playful elements are placed throughout the interior, from scattered colorful coat-hooks and a custom undercroft swing-bench. Sky House is thus rooted in a desire to accommodate personal domestic narratives as much as it is driven by a careful understanding of the site, and associated massing, programmatic, environmental, and material strategies.

*Sky House is rooted in a desire
to accommodate personal
domestic narratives.*

THE FARM

Scott Posno Design
Clarington, Ontario

Located an hour east of Toronto, adjacent to a large conservation forest, The Farm serves as a weekend and vacation home for the client, his grown children, and a variety of friends and family who frequent the tranquil property for relaxation and enjoyment year-round.

The Farm aims to engage the history and physical attributes of the site while amplifying a relationship with the outdoors. The main house sits atop a shallow ridge and its steeply gabled form and exaggerated length suggest a modern interpretation of the vernacular barn typology. The house is clad in cedar siding stained a soft charcoal, a perfect complement to the varied greens, browns, and grays of the landscape.

The luxurious double-height master suite enjoys a privileged position with a secluded patio, while the other two bedrooms are located on the second floor of the house. A separate loft space above the garage functions as both an artist's studio and self-contained guest suite.

The dining room occupies the full 22-foot (6-meter) width of the house and offers a flexibility of function: when the sliding glass pocket doors are closed, the room is a warm, intimate space for gathering; when the doors are slid open, it becomes not only an outdoor room, but a conduit linking front and back, interior and exterior, east and west.

Polished concrete floors in the public areas are balanced by an abundance of white oak used for millwork throughout, and for the stairs and flooring on the second level. The introduction of Douglas fir in the form of an expressed structural ceiling system is a reminder of the inherently rustic origins of the project.

South of the main house, a secondary zone focuses activity on an outdoor pool, hot tub, and a sunken firepit beneath another trellis. By night, in the darkness, stargazing becomes a favored nocturnal activity for those comfortably ensconced in the Adirondack chairs that ring the adjacent stone firepit.

The Farm aims to engage the history and physical attributes of the site while amplifying a relationship with the outdoors.

WOODHOUSE

superkül
Singhampton, Ontario

This striking house in the country near Singhampton, Ontario, was designed for a couple and their two children. Comprising an existing nineteenth-century log cabin and a modern addition, the house is sited in a large clearing on a heavily wooded site.

The two building forms are unified into a cohesive whole through the material expression of exterior cladding materials: riffing on the rough-hewn logs of the old cabin, charred wood siding is a modern interpretation that ensures visual and textural continuity. Similarly, a low gable roof was chosen for the new addition to reference the existing cabin as an integral compositional element of the scheme.

Entry into the small mudroom addition on the east side of the existing cabin—now converted into a large living room with guest bedrooms above—is the first stage in a linear sequence of spaces. Further on, the glazed corridor connects old with new. Within the modern addition, an exterior breezeway divides public and private functions, encouraging the residents to fully engage with the elements all year long. When the sliding doors are closed, a vaulted ceiling featuring a bank of four north-facing skylights opens up the space and refocuses attention from the horizontal plane of landscape beyond to the sky above, retaining an intimate connection to the natural world.

Sealed concrete comprises the flooring throughout most of the house, while interior walls and sculpturally articulated ceilings are sheathed in whitewashed birch plywood, reflecting the texture and tone of the raw wood interior of the existing log cabin. As the social heart of the house, the open-concept kitchen and dining area encourages relaxed interaction among family and guests.

The house reflects the affable and lively spirit of the family, embodied in the warm, textured material palette and a diversity of spatial conditions. Most importantly, to facilitate their insistence on an ever-present connection to the landscape, the architectural strategy prioritizes the seamless flow of interior and exterior spaces with as few visual, physical, and mechanical barriers to the experience of the home and property.

The house reflects the affable and lively spirit of the family, embodied in the warm, textured material palette and a diversity of spatial conditions.

BOWEN ISLAND HOUSE

Office of McFarlane Biggar Architects + Designers
Bowen Island, British Columbia

Bowen Island House is a calm, year-round retreat for a couple with young children seeking refuge from their busy professional lives. Nestled along the dramatic north shore of Bowen Island with its lush temperate rainforest, this modern, modest-sized cabin in the woods offers the basic pleasures of a contemporary home with deep connections to nature and a light environmental impact.

This cabin is an important, positive alternative to the prevailing trends of overdevelopment. The simple two-level volume, clad in local cedar and insulated glass, houses three bedrooms, two full bathrooms, and the open-plan kitchen, dining, and living area. Siting the house perpendicular to the rocky coastline helps diminish its presence, while capturing the rare sun from east and west.

True to its cabin ideals, the remote Bowen Island House is able to operate independently from the grid when necessary, with its own generator for use during extreme weather conditions. Under normal circumstances, the house is connected to the local hydroelectric power grid. All other services are completely off-grid, with fresh water supplied from a private well on the property and waste water treated on-site.

Cast-in-place concrete walls mediate between the mossy ground and the wood-framed elements above. Black-stained cedar cladding visually recedes into the forest. The green roof reinstates the absorptive qualities of the forest floor below the modest footprint, while glazed roof lanterns capture additional daylight and sun. Local hemlock floors and ceilings create warm interior spaces; expansive decks seamlessly integrate interior and exterior experience.

Connecting the architecture and nature, windows offer intimate views differing distinctively from the expansive views of the ocean; minimal frames help dematerialize the building skin while maximizing views and daylight. Holistically integrated throughout, the simple tectonic language and spatial clarity resonate with the surrounding coastal landscape, creating memorable architecture deeply rooted to its place.

This modern, modest-sized cabin in the woods offers the basic pleasures of a contemporary home with deep connections to nature and a light environmental impact.

HOUSE ON THE
BENCH _SA
Naramata, British Columbia

When the clients wanted to build a house that would boast lake views and a small vineyard, they approached _SA for advice. Happily, a site was located with various complexities but would prove perfect for the clients' needs.

The site consists of an open shallow slope that has become the vineyard while the lower portion drops off into a deep forested gorge where the Naramata Creek runs below. The house projects outward, reaching over the gorge with panoramic views toward Lake Okanagan to the west.

The remarkable qualities of the landscape and its surrounding context generated the conceptual strategy for this project. Because the site was originally neglected and deemed unusable for a house, the project embraces the existing site conditions and uses its unique qualities to create a heightened living experience for the client—a getaway overlooking the Okanagan Valley.

The home simultaneously exploits and respects the land. To achieve this delicate balance, the architects used a steel frame, material not typically used for residential application. The long, narrow house is laid between the gorge and the vineyard, effectively bridging the gap between the two aspects of the site. On the bench to the east of the site, grapevines are planted in a north/south orientation to maximize exposure to the sun for optimal growth. The design of the house parallels the vineyard, maximizing natural light into the home and views out to the lake.

One approaches the house by entering through a concrete wall, to arrive at a framed view of the primary entrance with the vineyard beyond, and ultimately the lake view opposite.

The garage/guest suite is separated from the main house by a loggia and covered outdoor living room that function as part of the house in summer weather. Procession within is through a sequence of tall spaces that embrace the lake, forest, and vineyard views. The enfilade of rooms becomes narrower and more private as it moves northward, culminating in the main bedroom that opens dramatically onto a cantilevered terrace vista overlooking the gorge and the rushing river below.

Procession within is through a sequence of tall spaces that embrace the lake, forest, and vineyard views.

Project Credits

Bowen Island House 188-97
Office of McFarlane Biggar
Architects + Designers · officemb.ca
Photography Ema Peter

Cap St-Martin Résidence 26-33
Bourgeois / Lechasseur architects · bourgeoislechasseur.com
Photography Adrien Williams

Cottage on the Point 34-43
Paul Bernier Architecte · paulbernier.com
Photography Raphaël Thibodeau

Ell House 110-17
Ravi Handa Architect · rha.works
in collaboration with **AAmp Studio** · aampstudio.com
Photography Maxime Brouillet

Go Home Bay Cabin 118-25
Ian MacDonald Architect · ima.ca
Photography Courtesy of Ian MacDonald Architect

Grand-Pic Chalet 44-51
APPAREIL architecture · appareilarchitecture.com
Photography Félix Michaud

House on the Bench 198-205
_SA · sturgessarchitecture.com
Photography Ema Peter

Kawagama Lake Boathouse 126-33
Building Arts Architects · buildingarts.ca
Photography David Whittaker

Lake Brome Residence 52-61
Atelier Pierre Thibault · pthibault.com
Photography Maxime Brouillet

Lake Joseph Cottage 134-43
VFA Architecture + Design · vf-a.com
Photography Cindy Blazevic

Lake Manitouwabing Residence 144-51
MJMA Architecture & Design · mjma.ca
Photography Shai Gil

Lake Mississauga Cottage 152-61
architects Tillmann Ruth Robinson · atrr.ca
Photography Jeanie Tam

Lakeside Cabin 62-69
Atelier Schwimmer · schwimmer.ca
Photography Adrien Williams

Laurentian Ski Chalet 70-77
RobitailleCurtis · robitaillecurtis.com
Photography Marc Kramer

Maison Perchée 78-85
Natalie Dionne Architecture · ndarchitecture.net
Photography Raphaël Thibodeau

May House 8-15
FBM · fbm.ca
Photography Julian Parkinson

Prefabricated Country Home 86-93
Figurr Architects Collective · figurr.ca
Photography David Boyer

Résidence St-Ignace 94-101
Nathalie Thibodeau architecte · ntarchitecte.ca
Photography Maxime Brouillet

Sky House 162-69
Julia Jamrozik and Coryn Kempster · ck-jj.com
Photography Doublespace Photography

Smith House 16-25
MacKay-Lyons Sweetapple Architects · mlsarchitects.ca
Photography Doublespace Photography

The Farm 170-79
Scott Posno Design · scottposno.com
Photography Doublespace Photography

The Slender House 102-9
MU Architecture · architecture-mu.com
Photography Stéphane Groleau

Woodhouse 180-87
superkül · superkul.ca
Photography Alex Fradkin / Kayla Rocca

Published in Australia in 2022 by
The Images Publishing Group Pty Ltd
ABN 89 059 734 431

Offices

Melbourne
6 Bastow Place
Mulgrave, Victoria 3170
Australia
Tel: +61 3 9561 5544

New York
6 West 18th Street 4B
New York City, NY 10011
United States
Tel: +1 212 645 1111

Shanghai
6F, Building C, 838 Guangji Road
Hongkou District, Shanghai 200434
China
Tel: +86 021 31260822

books@imagespublishing.com
www.imagespublishing.com

Copyright © The Images Publishing Group Pty Ltd 2022
The Images Publishing Group Reference Number: 1599

All photography is attributed in the Project Credits on page 206 unless otherwise noted.
Pages 2–3: Cindy Blazevic (VFA Architecture + Design, Lake Joseph Cottage); page 4:
Maxime Brouillet (Atelier Pierre Thibault, Lake Brome Residence); page 7: Cindy Blazevic
(VFA Architecture + Design, Lake Joseph Cottage); page 206: Ema Peter (_SA, House on
the Bench)

A catalogue record for this
book is available from the
National Library of Australia

Title: Northern Hideaways: Canadian Cottages and Cabins
Author: Julia Jamrozik [Introduction]
ISBN: 9781864709063

This title was commissioned in IMAGES' Melbourne office and produced as follows:
Editorial Georgia (Gina) Tsarouhas, Jeanette Wall *Graphic design* Ryan Marshall
Production Nicole Boehringer

Printed on 157gsm Chinese OJI FSC® matt art paper, by Artron Art (Group) Co., Ltd, in China

IMAGES has included on its website a page for special notices in relation to this and its
other publications. Please visit www.imagespublishing.com

Every effort has been made to trace the original source of copyright material contained in
this book. The publishers would be pleased to hear from copyright holders to rectify any
errors or omissions.

The information and illustrations in this publication have been prepared and supplied by
the architects and contributors. While all reasonable efforts have been made to ensure
accuracy, the publishers do not, under any circumstances, accept responsibility for errors,
omissions and representations express or implied.